An empowered organization is one in which
individuals have the knowledge, skill, desire, and
opportunity to personally succeed in a way that
leads to collective organizational success.
- Stephen R. Covey

What if your people led regardless of the role they
hold in your organization?

What if your people wanted to take part in change
initiatives?

What if professional development left your people
with a practical route forward?

Leadership coaching is the essential tool for
changing an organization. As you know, change is
fundamental for organizations to grow and adjust
for today's transient shifting marketplace, yet people
and organizations are immune to change.
Leadership coaching can hasten efficacious changes
in teams, employees and systems by clarifying
visions, beliefs, values, strengthening knowledge and
enabling leaders, managers and employees to
uncover their full potential.

Coaching people can help them to eliminate the
consequences of negative emotions such as fear -

the most inhibitive feeling, guilt and worry. Fear is the most important emotion that you have to change because it can influence your personal life and your career, keeping you away from challenges and accomplishments.

To coach people you firstly need to be an efficient leader with vision, determination, integrity, motivation in order to improve and encourage people, strong and effective communication skills and positive thinking and what is the most important- empathy.

Nowadays, coaching has become a booming niche of development because the business environment is a competitive arena where everyone is struggling for their purposes and dreams, jobs are more complex than in the past, the challenges are more complicated, rapid changes arise every moment, organizations have to understand and solve people's issues and needs.

Chapter 1: Leadership as a blending of strategy and character

Blending character and strategy is the best approach in leadership. Strategy helps a leader know the prevailing situation and how to best work toward bettering the status quo. Both strategy and character are equally important in leadership. Since neither of them should be given higher priority because they are all important, they ought to be mixed in a balanced way. Therefore, this piece explores the reasons why any chartered and accomplished leader/coach must have both.

Even with the best strategy, a leader cannot discharge his responsibilities without a formidable character and personality. In many organizations, you will find very bright and able leaders who cannot lead simply because they have given their reputation/character to the dogs. Employees who do not hold their boss in high esteem, for example, cannot take them seriously even when their ideas are for everyone's good. That is why a leader must have both good strategy and a personality that is beyond reproach.

Strategy is born of a superior brain and character is born out of the richness of one's soul. In this case, a seasoned leader needs both a good personality and a strong character. This helps him convince those under them about what should be done in every situation. His experience/wisdom/knowledge comes in handy in designing the strategy. This way, he is able to win the support of those under him. However, for him to have the support of their subordinates, he ought to have won his confidence as well. It is however not possible to win the confidence of your subordinates unless they know that you are a person of a good-natured and well-meaning personality.

It is said that a superior brain may take you to the heavens but it takes a sound character to stay there. A good leader who charts wonderful strategies that can take an organization to the clouds should also have the requisite character to maintain it there. In some situations, especially in a crisis, very stringent measures that require a lot of discipline to execute are needed. In this regard, the strategies are of little use without the availability of the required personality on the part of the leader/coach.

In conclusion, it is impossible to succeed as a leader/coach without a perfect balance between character and strategy. The first one is the engine that moves the locomotive of leadership while the latter is the wheel. Neither can be of any use without the perfect balance of the two.

Chapter 2: Fundamental traits for being a leader

A leader is a person given mandate to head, direct or represent others in a given field. Leadership is such an important role that has power and responsibility bestowed upon him or her. A leader must present and conduct himself to the public in a way that will build good rapport and relations to the audience.

A leader should therefore possess certain traits and characters that are the key in discharging the duties of service to others. These behavioral characteristics not only help the leader but also make those he leads to have confidence in him. These qualities are illustrated below.

Adjustment

It is the ability to change or to improve in order to adapt in the constantly changing environment. A leader should therefore be flexible enough to a state that best suits and is favorable to the willing majority. He or she must act in a way that is considered correct by the members of the group. It is mainly applied in problem solving and coordinating the efforts of the members to work together.

Charisma

It is the capability of influencing a large group being able to introduce new ideas and ways of doing things. The leader is able to achieve this without creating ill feelings among the people. Such a behavior is the manner in which the leader conducts himself or herself. It must be in a manner that is descent and socially acceptable.

Extraversion

It is a rare trait that any leader who is focused towards excellence is required to embrace. It is the power of being happy in company of others as opposed to be being alone. A leader cannot coordinate others of he or she is not able to associate with them by being social, assertive and talkative to understand there deep feelings and opinions of the organization.

Intelligence

Intelligence also comes handy when leaders are mentioned at any forum. As a leader you should have the ability to acquire and apply knowledge and skills. You should be able to acquire the latest technics that are key in service delivery and in line with the visions and goals of the organization. It also demands a high capacity of the leader to learn and relate with the daily life experiences.

As discussed above the golden rules of leadership include charisma, extraversion, intelligence, adjustment and behavior. These traits when combined with many others in a leader he or she will be a leader for people.

Chapter 3: Learning the foundations of leadership

Leadership is often taken for granted but in fact it is not as simple as most people think. That is why some people excel in leadership while others fail. The presence of many leadership theories is a testament that it is a subject that has presented a challenge and thus elicited the contribution of different scholastic schools of thought. All these theories seem to endeavor to demystify leadership and make it understandable to many.

As such, this piece explores the Four Core Theory Groups approach in leadership. To begin with, the Trait Theory is among the four group theories. This theory ordains that people succeed in leading while others fail because of their different personalities. Many of the early trait theories held that leadership is innate and that people could do nothing to be good leadership unless they were with the intrinsic abilities of a leader.

However, contemporary trait theories show that leadership is an art that can be perfected. Behavioral Theories are also part of the four core theory group. This kind of leadership study looks into how leaders behave or how they should behave. For instance, should leaders dictate what should be done and expect the unanimous cooperation of members or should they involve them in the decision making process and then chart out the way forward together? Under this category, there are three cadres of leaders.

First, there are autocratic leaders who are despots who lead dictatorially. Again, there are democratic leaders who encourage team work and equal participation. Laissez-faire leaders also fall in this class and this is kind of leadership whereby subordinates are given the leeway to think on their won and execute their responsibilities as they deem fit.

Another among the four core theory group is the contingency theory that ordains that leaders behave the way they do because of the prevailing circumstances or situations. However, it has met a lot of acrid opposition from other schools of thought since it was widely believed that it is during a crisis that the true quality and character of leadership is tried and fire-furnaced.

The last of these theories is the Power and Influence Theories approach. This view of leadership analysis stipulates that a leader acts depending on the amount of power, mandate, or ambit under their jurisdiction.

For instance, how much power a leader has is thought to profoundly affect how they push their subordinates to get things done?

Chapter 4: Essence of Self-motivation in leadership

Self-motivation is the force that drives and aids you to do things by yourself without being supervised, monitored, or forced to do them. It is the inner feeling that keeps one encouraged and going. While working towards achievement of the set goals, missions, and visions self-motivation is a very crucial virtue that any leader should have in order to effectively serve the people they are in charge of and achieve the goals they intend during their tenure.

First, self-motivation helps a leader develop a sense of positive attitude and development. A self-motivated leader shall always develop a good attitude and perception towards his responsibilities mandated to discharge. A positive attitude enhances effectiveness and hard work in a leader.

Secondly, self-motivation paves the way for the leader to be self-empowered and self- developed. This is a situation where a leader improves the quality of their leadership through experience while discharging the duties. Leadership is a career that entails much issues and roles. The leader usually deals with numerous problems as they carry out their duties. Through interaction with new people and situations they understand ways of doing things a leader gains new knowledge and ideas on how to deal with various issues such as proper and effective evaluation and implementation of ideas and judgment. Consequently, a leader develops their self-worth.

Moreover, self-motivation helps a leader increase and improve the morale working of the junior employees who work under their supervision. The employees work to their utmost if the leader works as an example and role model to them. The junior employees shall only be encouraged to work harder and smarter if the leadership also performs and discharges its duties as required. As a result, teamwork, solidarity, and unity are enhanced. This in return creates an opportunity for the success of not only the employees but also the leader and the organization as a whole.

The art of personal organization in leadership also comes as a result of self-motivation. A self-motivated leader shall be able to finish the task assigned to do and attend to the roles in time.

Leadership entails the setting, achievement, and fulfillment of the goals by either the leader or the organization they are is in charge of. Realistic goals shall only be set and accomplished if the leader is self-motivated.

It is said that inner drive and desire that shall keep the leader are moving towards accomplishing the set goals, objectives and missions of an organization.

Chapter 5: Why should you be an authentic leader?

It is wise to keep a notch higher by realizing the pros and cons of being authentic as a leader. Becoming an authentic leader will require little effort but, more practice and enough patience. Here are qualities common to famous authentic leaders.

Being unique is what will attract the attention of multitudes and make their thinking fit with your own objectives. Furthermore, the similar the objectives the clearer the goals and faster the period spent convincing fellows who have different views towards life to work together.

Authenticity makes a leader be strictly objective minded. Being objective-minded is crucial because it brings you to a position of mobilizing dozens of individuals to a common goal, go ahead and state your goal and define it clearly. This will create a self-driven environment which is not only productive but one that also reduces expensive hustles in supervising and snoopy guidance to irresponsible individuals.

Authenticity encourages practicality. With practicality, people are able to pragmatically link the issues at hand with the situation on the ground. No matter how serious attention your objectives need, it is wise to look out of the box and relate the matter at hand with current issues that many can identify with, and this will include the political and economic perspectives of the day. Any steps taken towards solving any problem are out of touch and are as useless as deodorized dog-shit.

The level of your authenticity will clearly define your knowledge too, so get your proof and supporting evidence from trusted resources, and where possible, have it as your original idea. These make you reliable, and stand out in a crowd of copycats. As such, being authentic helps you expand your field of knowledge. When people face hardships, they are forced to think beyond the box and thus expand their intelligence antennae and thus impart more knowledge upon themselves. Since they are not willing to just borrow leaves carelessly, they embark on painstaking research in bid to come up with novel solutions to emerging problems.

Authenticity motivates transparency. A leader who is authentic in his leadership has nothing to hide. And yes, you should have nothing to hide, get your ego out there and put across your message in the best way that suits you and your subordinates. Let your directions lead others, have your voice acted upon and let yourself be the best you've always wanted to be.

Chapter 6: Ethical leadership
Doing the Right Thing

Ethical leadership is important. You can imagine being led by a leader who lacks commendable ethics. Leadership is only for those who have the ability to present themselves as role models to the rest. If you can't be an epitome of irreproachable ethics, then you have no business leading. As such, this piece explores the profound benefits of being an ethical leader.

To begin with, an ethical leader who practices impregnable ethics is able to command the respect of their followers. It is impossible to people who do not hold you in high esteem. The reason why any leader receives the unquestionable respect of their subordinates is because they sought to lead by example. It would be myopic to hope to win the respect of those under you if you have not shown respect to them by upholding the requisite painstaking ethics.

Again, being an ethical leader helps one understand the feeling of those under them. By choosing to be ethical yourself and understanding your subordinates makes you inspire a sense of motivation. With followers who feel appreciated and understood, the leader has a better chance to rule and lead with grace. The reward of understanding those under you is having them understand you as well. And any leader should be happy having subordinates who understand him.

Thirdly, an ethical leader is able to cultivate friendship with their subordinates. Psychologists have shown that people are naturally rebellious and they easily may choose to disobey while knowing that they will be punished any way. However, they have been able to show that it is not easy for people to wrong their friends. The punishment brought by breaking the law is not as deterrent as the mental guilt of wronging a friend. With this, they have succeeded in proving that the best way to win the obedience is becoming their friends.

Lastly, an ethical leader is able to create an atmosphere of camaraderie. When the boss loves and appreciates all those under them, they motivate them to love and become better friends among themselves. The opposite is quite true. A leader who does not love and appreciate their employees causes strife among them and makes them start treating each other with contempt and suspicion.

Define your organization's value

To lead people with character and integrity, you must set an example. You are the leader, remember? And your team follows you because you represent that authority and integrity they need in order to guide their actions. First, you need to understand yourself, your own values as well as the organization's values.

As an example, the global technology giant 3M is famous for its company values.

Why? Because the team-from top executive managers to the mailroom- live for the concepts of honesty and integrity every day. 3M defines clearly that it expects staff to keep promises, have personal accountability and respects others in the workforce. Every leader knows this and works following these rules. As a result, everyone else follows.

As a leader, it is your duty to set rules and codes and to make sure that you enforce them.

Your personal values are very important in your work as a leader, because you can define what's most important in your life. Your values should determine your priorities and, deep down, they probably are the measures you use to determine if your life is turning out the way you want to.

Their absence brings ambiguity and can be a real source of unhappiness.

That's why you need to make a conscious effort to identify your values and their importance.

How Values Help You

Values exist even if we don't recognize them or we don't accept them. When you manage to acknowledge them, your life catches that shapes you dreamt. Making plans and taking decisions become easier. Questions like these will definitely help you to make decisions in life:

- What job should I pursue?
- Should I accept this promotion?
- Should I start my new business?
- Should I compromise, or be form with my position?
- Should I follow tradition, or travel down a new path?

You have the answer and it will help you understand your real priorities and you will be able to take the right direction and accomplish your life goals.

In conclusion, a leader who aspires to present a strong ethical personality motivates their followers to be ethical as well. With this transparency, accountability, and integrity sweep across the entire organization.

Chapter 7: Perceiving the true meaning of power

Power is the ability to influence others towards accomplishing a certain goal. The ability of a leader to influence the activities of others is what may be defined as power. Leadership is based on power without which it cannot exist.

Position power is one described by the job title where one works. It is vested to a leader by the organization to exercise it on behalf of the administrators.

A different form of power is personal power. It is power vested to a leader by other people. It is an indication of the commitment the subordinates have towards their leader. It is followed and strengthened by the people's belief that the leader has the legitimacy to give them instructions that they will eventually follow.

When a leader possesses qualities that followers admire, is created referent power. Followers maybe noticed trying to imitate or copy their leader in various ways. Referent power varies form one leader to another. Some wield influence over a small number of people, while others have admiration from over millions, through their charisma and personality.

Leaders have various forms of wielding power. There are those who exercise their power over others when they don't do what is required of them. They impose penalties on such individuals, taking various forms ranging from verbal abuse, demotion from job position or even withdrawal of privileges.

In the above case the followers believe that the leader is capable of imposing a penalty of his choice to the subjects. For it to be effective it must be something that the followers do not enjoy going through. It should be a penalty that affects the targeted follower directly, for example, a ban on tobacco will not affect a non-smoker.

When a leader makes it a routine to reward his subjects when they meet his expectations, he tends to wield some degree of power over them. They always do things the best way possible so that they may be rewarded at the end of the task.

As such, it must be a reward that is appealing to the followers for them to view it as an incentive. For the leader to be perceived as powerful, he must be dependable. He must be someone who fulfills his promise.

It is crucial that the reward offered is proportionate to the task the subject has completed. If the reward is way smaller than the task completed, the subject may feel undervalued. Good leaders know how to build power around their followers. They do not need to command it but rather comes out on its own.

Chapter 8: Emotional intelligence is a binder between leadership and coaching

Many people may have an understanding of other forms of intelligence but they may not be quite familiar with emotional intelligence. Emotional intelligence is a pivotal ingredient that every accomplished leader should have. As such, this article explores the importance and definition of emotional intelligence in leadership and leadership coaching.

Emotional intelligence is the ability to manage your own emotions and those of others. It includes three major skills. The first one is the kind of emotional awareness that identifies one's emotions and those of others. The second aspect involves the ability to harness your emotions and those of others and applying them in solving the problems at hand. The third aspect is about regulating your own emotions and also the knack to help others handle their emotions.

With that said, how does emotional intelligence act as the binder between leadership and coaching? To begin with, a leader and coach who are able to identify their own emotions are in an excellent position to take the necessary steps to act on them. For instance, a leader/coach who knows that they are tempered will not let their temper ruin their good influence on their subordinates/trainees. Any coach/leader that has emotional awareness of their negative emotions will rule them and enhance the coach-trainee relationship for better results.

Further, a leader/coach who understands and is able to identify the emotions of others is able to handle them in a way that does not motivate the undesirable emotions in them. Even when the negative emotions emerge in a particular subordinate or trainee, the coach/leader who is emotionally intelligence will know how to take control of the situation. During the coaching process, the trainees have to be taught the importance of emotional intelligence in leadership. Since it is impossible for anyone to teach what they do not know, it is imperative that the coaches themselves understand what emotional intelligence is way before they start coaching others about it.

Finally, we all know how emotions affect the way we respond to situations. Any seasoned leader/coach knows when to apply the prevailing emotional climate in order to achieve helpful milestones. Some regrettable emotional blunders may sometimes happen. Instead of blaming hell for such developments, any good leader takes charge of the situation and converts the weakness into strength. For instance, when everyone is bitter because things have gone terribly wrong, it is not the time for blame-gaming but the best time to address the underlying triggers of the problem in order to thwart any chances of its future occurrence, and any qualified leader knows this.

Chapter 9: Adaptability is a crucial skill for an agile leader and the key for coaching

Any agile leader must be adaptable and should be able to make their followers adaptable as well. However, it is not easy to achieve adaptability. As such, this piece explores some benefits and tips of being an adaptable leader.

To begin with, a leader who is adaptable should be able to listen and understand those they lead. The whole rationale behind enhancing one's adaptability as leader is about studying the disposition of the people they are leading and do several adjustments in order to reach them better.

It is said that you should behave like a Roman when you go to Rome. The greatest advantage of leading people that you know and adapt yourself to the peculiar situation at hand is that you are able to avoid some obvious pitfalls that would have otherwise remained obscure. It does not save time but money as well. Interacting with the people you lead in an attempt to know them also cultivates friendship and a sense of camaraderie.

Further, an adaptable leader should be able domesticate ideas and policies. Despite which leadership school you attended and whatever lofty ideologies you learned there, you should be able to domesticate the leadership ideas you learned in school. The advantage of domesticating your ideas is that it achieves better results. Since little goes to waste in terms of resources and time, money and power are markedly saved.

Adaptable leaders also have the capacity to draw from their wealth of experience and take charge of the situation at hand. There is a famous saying that history has an invariable tendency to repeat itself. As such, whatever happens in a particular situation has probably happened in another. An adaptable leader can thus relate a present crisis with another that happened in the past and borrow a leaf from the past.

The beauty of being a visionary and adaptable leader is that nothing is ever beyond your control as a leader. Another benefit is that originality takes center stage. Adaptable leaders do not follow rigidly set steps for solving a problem. They pragmatically go to the ground and try to substantiate the facts as they are. Armed with these facts, they are full able to engineer real-time solutions that make sense. On the other hand, leaders who have poor adaptability are unable to get themselves habituated to the present crisis and they tend to continue advancing ideas that do not work. This only leads to one big failure to another.

Chapter 10: Coaching as a meta-profession

Leadership coaching has become necessary in various fields of management. Workforce need to be equipped with skills that will enhance their output as well as their interaction with one another at the work place. Resources to be used for training by the coach are very vital. They should be carefully picked in order to ensure the set goals that have been achieved. A frame work needs to be set up such that to be able to evaluate oneself with the progress the coaches are making. A physical therapy with pre-requisite training technique uses the latest principles of coaching. This should be aimed at mentoring to upgrade posture through body awareness.

Efficient tools of coaching that revolve around guidance, support and strategies that help create a conducive environment and to improve the perception of learners are of a mandatory importance. In the event that a manager gets concerned by a demotivated workforce, sometimes a pay rise may not be the solution but rather coaching the workforce on social techniques that they need to employ while with each other. Teamwork is number one if outstanding results are part of the expectations in any organization. In the coaching process, coaches need to identify forms of self-limiting decisions resourceful emotions and sometimes beliefs that tend to disfigure the focus of an individual in their struggle to accomplishing their goals.

It takes real hard work to become what we want or rather what we ought to be. This is largely contributed by the fact that we are all born into an unsympathetic world where success is hardly won. Self-empowerment coupled by personal development and a general coaching education is a mandatory ingredient in the success recipe.

Consultations are in most cases a positive input to effective management and in other cases to improve the existing quality of output. Organizational development and professional leadership are the most important aspects in the practice and theory of management.

Upcoming coaches need to re-evaluate themselves by observing how more experienced coaches carry out themselves. Coaching is a very sensitive profession as one needs to carry him/herself with care to avoid killing the dream or the morale of a coach. Once one goes through these induction activities, they develop collective understanding and share in the meanings of different occupation culture as the coaching goes on. As time goes, the coach is able to identify key areas that need more emphasis in their coaches, so that they are able to disseminate the same knowledge to their workforce or target group.

Chapter 11: Golden rules of coaching

Leadership coaching does not just go about lectures. It entails much more than that. First, one needs to identify the problem but rather to coach the person so that their skills to handle the problem and similar ones that may arise in future are enhanced. For the real power to be bought out vividly, it needs to come from deep within for it to bring sustainable change.

The coach needs to be at the service of the client. The coach needs to put his ego aside and listen and sometimes silence the client, be direct and supportive. A little play and some rudeness' may also be blended well so that it breaks the monotony of the topic at hand.

The choices we make are far more reaching than we sometimes think. Things people say or do and sometimes the emotions expressed sometimes express much more about ourselves. Coaching clients makes them open up only to realize that they are even more resourceful than and with the resources around them. This helps them to accomplish their visions and goals. Challenges start becoming possibilities.

Clients need to stricken with a sense of humor to make them get to the creative side of their brains. Playfulness and stillness help the coach get to their own focus too. Effective coaching revolves around aspects such as shaping the future. The future should not only be envisioned but also created. Ideas need to be tested against existing resources.

Making things happen is leaders' number one priority. They must have a way of converting strategies into action. An effective leader knows how to assign accountability and which decisions to manage and which to delegate and ensuring teamwork in the process.

Any leader looks forward to optimizing his team's performance. This can only be achieved by bringing out the best in the people. Talent must be built and engaged for immediate results to be achieved. Building the next generation is a key aspect in leadership. People, competence and human-capital developers are required for strategic success in the future.

Investing in oneself is the key in the leadership model one wants to offer. A leader cannot influence others unless he has created time and energy in self-awareness enhancement of personal attributes that will go hand-in-hand with what the followers expect of him. An effective leader is pace-setting, participative, affiliative and visionary. However leaders have different preferred styles of leadership, blending both soft and hard approaches, yet blending the two in the management of tasks and caring for peoples' concerns.

Chapter 12: The power of coaching

Coaching people in leadership is not an easy venture. It is tantamount to being a teacher in which case one has to know what they are teaching before they stand before the learners. Read on to discover a few tips that are going to help you as you embark on leadership coaching.

One of the surefire tips to guide when doing leadership coaching is engaging all the parties involved. You must desist from engaging in an endless monologue that does not seek to incorporate all the parties involved. If you cannot succeed in getting all the participants while coaching, then you better stop doing it. Ensure that the whole team is alert and motivated. This means that the person doing the coaching should be a savvy mind that can detect when some team members are withdrawn or left out.

Moreover, a leadership coach has to be as practical as possible. Note that all the people you are coaching spent a lot of time in school and they therefore have no interest in being subjecting to the rigmaroles of formal class work. You should always begin by being as practically motivational as possible. Right from the start underscore the benefits of the coaching and the kind of helpful skills the trainees are going to have at the end of the session. By making the process as informal as possible and fun oriented, you are going to doubtless win the attention and goodwill of the learners.

Quote examples of prosperous people the learners are familiar with and ones who have benefited from similar coaching. This gives them a mental image of how they are going to be once they complete the coaching session. You may also elucidate how you have benefited from similar tutorials in the past and how they fundamentally changed your life. This makes those being coached plucked the requisite morale to continue with the coaching process. Again, it makes them take the whole undertaking positively, leading to better results.

Finally, you should drop any schoolmasterly attitude toward the people you are coaching. Being already a leader yourself, you must teach others how to mingle with other people gracefully. Make it a platform for equal participation. Ask questions and challenge your audience to offer practical answers. You must try to avoid imposing your opinions on your trainees. Make the session trainee-oriented since it is not you learning but them. Encourage authenticity and originality throughout the whole process.

Chapter 13: The grow model - why do we need to be a leader to coach people?

It is a pipedream to hope to lead others when you are not a leader yourself. It is like teaching Greek to other people if you do not know it yourself. As such it pays to master your craft first before you can start teaching it to others. Therefore, this piece underscores some aspects of true leadership that those acting as leadership coaches must acquaint themselves with. Read on to discover more.

A true coach needs to be a leader who teaches their trainees to outline their leadership goals. Setting clear goals while everyone is groping in the darkness is the very acme of good leadership and anyone coaching people on leadership must be very familiar with this. With this knowledge and ability, they will be able to motivate their trainees to have the same abilities.

A true leader who qualifies to be coach needs to have a clear vision to see the future and also one who has eyes for the current situation. This is because the future cannot exist without today because the present moment is a bridge of the future. Those learning useful leadership tips must familiarize themselves with this aspect of leadership. As such, only a seasoned leader who has perfected the art of deciphering the present moment will have the adroitness to lead others. A leadership coach must therefore be a qualified leader for himself.

A true leader and coach must teach his trainers that every good leader must always consider all the options at their disposal when tackling a problem. For the trainees to understand how a qualified leader weighs up a situation and comes up with options on how to get out of the mayhem, they ought to be taught by a chartered leader who has practically done it before.

Further, any leadership coach must be himself a good leader who underscores the essence of a strong will. How can one coach others to have a strong will when leading while they have not practiced it before himself. Yes, a leadership coach must be a leader who has used strong will in their past positions of leadership.

Finally, any leadership coach must be himself a leader who understands the essence of charting out the way forward despite how gloomy this look. So how can you tell people to always come up with a way forward while in a crisis while you have not done it yourself? A leader must be a doyen in the field who has practically implemented the skills they teach.

Chapter 14: Create a high performance team

The reason why corporations cave in is not because the chairs are not of the best quality or because the floors are not glossy-tiled. They collapse because the people steering their wheels are not visionary enough. A visionary leader is not the one who relies on their own abilities because they cannot be in charge of every department. You must learn how to delegate tasks as a leader. And for delegation to work, one needs to have a highly motivated army of team members who are not only equipped with the right skills but also ones who have the right attitude.

As such, this piece explores a number of tips to nurture a team of highly motivated staff. Three cardinal aspects of creating a powerful team that are discussed below are: building strong relationships, nurturing accountability, and doing excellent networking. Read on.

1. How to Nurture Strong Relationship

Nurturing strong professional relationship is not easy as a leader. First, it is imperative to ensure that your subordinates do not view you as the big boss'. Instead, they should see you as a fellow team member who is only the captain of the crew. Instead of inspiring fear, you should engineer a sense of mutual respect, understand, and a strong feeling of camaraderie/fellowship. Know everyone and let them know themselves. Any organization should have a well-rounded distribution of skills and competences. Tap into everyone's strongest points and boost productivity as you cultivate a sense of cordial friendliness.

2. The Importance of Accountability

Any organization that does not have a clear chain of accountability is bound to fail. Although self-accountability has to be the principal motivation, everyone cannot be left to their own devices. As such, people have to know who are above them and who are below them. The overall goal of this arrangement is not to inspire fear but make people aware of how tasks should be executed. When followers know that that there is a strong chain of accountability, they will be kept on track since they know that any blunder will be soon unmasked and the necessary steps taken.

3. The Benefits of Networking

Many people know the importance external networking but may not be very familiar with internal networking. When networking is encouraged, people are able to enlist the insight of others when tackling particularly thorny professional or technical jigsaws. Since there is never a new problem, networking enables employees to tap into the experience of their counterparts which have faced similar hurdles before.

Chapter 15: The power of trust and developing self-awareness

A popular adage ordains that trust is like virginity, once it is broken it cannot be broken it cannot be re-acquired. As such, it pays handsomely to engineer trust in all our dealings with other people. Those that have experienced the tremendous benefits will do anything to cement and maintain it.

In the same vein, self-awareness is as important as one's life. A person who has a high sense of self-awareness knows itself and does not need to rely on the other sources to know who they really are. Contrariwise, people who lack self-knowledge are like a sea vessel that is being buffeted from one end of the ocean to the other by wild tempestuous winds.

As such, this article underscores the importance of trust and self-awareness. Read on to discover why a leader should have these two.

The Power Of trust

Trust is so powerful. It is especially so crucial to a leader than any other person. To begin with, a leader who enjoys the trust of those below him has their respect. Since a leader should have the ability to see ahead of the pack and put in place some sound mechanisms to boost preparedness, they need to have the trust of the followers so that they can accept to follow them. The followers cannot see the future as clearly as the leader. As such, they do not know what should be done to prepare for that future. The leader knows what should be done. For the subordinates to accept what the leader tells them, they have to have the feeling that the leader is acting in their best interests as well as those of the organization.

The Essence of Developing Self Awareness

Having underscored the importance of self-awareness in the second paragraph, it is important to note that self-awareness does not happen in an instance, it is developed. Therefore, a leader should have a lofty sense of self-knowledge just like the followers should. However, a leader who does not know himself cannot help the subordinates to discover themselves. Although long, any leader worth the name must be willing to embark on the arduous journey to self-discovery. Set off, by asking yourself: "What are my strengths?" Then, "What are my weak points?"

Note that your weaknesses are as important as your strengths. As such, you must not be a narcissistic perfectionist who decidedly blinds his eyes on their weaknesses. Our weaknesses are just as important as our strong points. Know them!

Chapter 16: Empathy - the tool for building people into groups

Empathy is an often misunderstood term. It is perhaps the most advanced skill in communication. Empathy is defined as the ability to see the world through another person's eyes, in other words, putting oneself in the shoes of others. It involves understanding another person's feelings, emotional state, and concerns.

Empathy is a selfless act that helps us understand other people and create fraternal bonds with them. As such, people who are empathetic towards others are not just friends but soul mates. Having understood what empathy is, how can it help people form workable professional groups within an organization?

To begin with, people must not be groups simply because the supervisors have told them to coalesce into such units. For true work group to work, leader must understand his subordinates and empathy can help him attain this. Once the leader understands those under him, he is in a better position to help them. Although empathy is an advanced communication weapon that many people lack, it is relieving to know that people must not be necessarily born with it since it can be cultivated or developed in people. As such, it is the onus of a great leader to create empathy among his subordinates and lead by example. It is his business to nurture empathy and steer feasible group work within the organization.

Again, a leader who lacks empathy would treat the divergent opinions of others as arrant nonsense. On the other hand, a leader who is empathetic towards others would not brush off their ideas. Instead, he would try to understand why other people choose to think the way they do. Once you understand the underlying principles or experiences that motivate another person's viewpoint, you are able to concur with them. However funny or bizarre others' ideas may sound, they have something that can help you shape your own vision. Even better, various opinions/ideas on the same subject should merge to form a superior opinion/amicable way forward. And since a leader should be the most tolerant member of the team, he must acquire and practice empathy.

Finally, any leader who cares for the organization must know that empathy creates a true sense of friendship and mutual respect within a group. Any group that lacks these two can only be a waste of time. Friendly people who respect each another tend to take each other's ideas positively and they try to learn at least something from them. When people within a group are ready to receive divergent opinions positively and broad-mindedly, group members can only have the sky as their limit!

Chapter 17: Authenticity - a key to brand success

It is disheartening to see the world so full of mimicry. People have given their originality to the dogs and have chosen to be copycats. You are the best person the world has ever known and you should love your original ideas. As such, it is more than suicidal to embrace other's ideas and write off your original own. True leaders value authenticity and originality because they know that these are the engines to building a powerful brand name. As such, this piece explores the importance of authenticity when promoting a brand. Three aspects of authenticity will be expounded. Read on to discover more.

Authenticity is Self Definition

The worst thing about copying others and shunning being your original self is that you lose yourself definition. It is even ironical to copy others yet you want to be the champion in industry. If you are doing what your rivals in the trade, then how will you attain the difference that should help you cut a niche of excellence and be a cut above the rest? It is heavily satirical to run a race at the pace of other runners and hope to cross the end line ahead of them. It is tantamount to eating ones cake and then hope to still have it.

Therefore true leaders should go for authentic and original ideas that make them stand out of the clutter. Any you won't stand out of it unless you acquire yourself some measure of uniqueness. You should however note that the decision to chase uniqueness is a double-edged sword. You may chase uniqueness and self-definition for own sake until you lose sight of what you exactly like to achieve with your uniqueness.

Authenticity and Transparency Are Inseparable

A leader who embraces authenticity while promoting their brand also attains a good measure of transparency. Note that copycats cannot be fully transparent. Whether it is to one's subordinates or the outside public, authenticity cultivates a general sense of transparency. Transparency in turn inspires respect and confidence of those around you.

Therefore, you should always strive to be original and authentic as leader. Note that choosing to follow the path of authenticity is not easy. It is the bold step that you must be willing to take. Contrariwise, mimicry is a luring path that may look promising but it is a short road that ends quickly.

You must shun its easy lures and pay the cost of reaming boldly authentic.

Chapter 18: Coaching leadership style

Leadership may be described as process or ability to motivate or direct others. When a manager is working as a coach, he is certainly helping those whom he works with to improve on their skills and performance at work.

There are many times when we analyze our performance track we realize that there exists gaps in willpower and self-discipline that end up holding us back. High-performance coaching helps people identify and explore their motivation and overcome the blockers that deter them from achieving progress in the activities they are involved in.

Featuring this, evidence galore has shown that people with long term goals end up being successful than those without. There are many times when one is seen as primarily a holder of a position like that of a manager, but also to be seen as a leader; one who offers genuine inspiration and clear guidance. One needs to navigate through these roles tactfully in order to achieve an intellectual distinction in his/her company or even at the workplace.

There is an ultimate need for one to quit habitual moves and instead embrace relearning basic skills in the right way. This creates a calm atmosphere for self-development in leadership. Some life's setbacks tend to prevent one from achieving their set goals. High-performance training is very effective in dealing with such occurrences of stress and burnout in life.

Depending on our perceived difficulty of challenges, this model shows the emotional state that one is likely to experience when trying to accomplish various tasks. One of the aims of the coach should be help the learner get confident with the skills needed to achieve his goals in life or in a set duration of time.

Some fears are a reality while others are just a mind-play of negative tricks on us to be safe. A coach needs to take some time to deal with a trainee's fear of situations or action. Once he identifies them and discusses them, the power in them is broken and weakened. Still, a coach needs to take face the eventualities of life with courage to avoid distress.

When one is unable to accomplish tasks repeatedly, a tendency to feel guilt may overcome one and may actually kill their morale to do things. Some people get afraid over virtually everything and have little ability to overcome their worries. Coaches can help such individuals by openly discussing their worries which ends up weakening the impact they cause to the trainees.

High performance coaching not only challenges the trainees but also supports them in developing the levels they are able to attain a happy and successful career.

Conclusion

In the end I hope you understood that coaching is leading. Once you are mastering the tools of leadership, you will find that coaching is the most powerful form of leadership you can practice. Leaders with the proper coaching skills can motivate direct reports and work with bosses and peers in a manner that reduces dissensions and enhances productivity.

Today, more and more organizations are using coaching to increase performance and expound talent at each level. It will motivate employees and increase engagement, build the capacity for self-direction, facilitate team performance, address performance issues, improve peer relationships and practices.

Why do you need leadership coaching today?

In this changing global economy, the ability to implement change and strengthen performance is an essential leadership coaching skill.

1. Create your vision- Leading change

    It increases the awareness of your leadership
    coaching strengths as well as gets in the way of using
    those strengths in difficult situations. It solidifies
    your skills in your default leadership style. It shapes
    the components of a strong vision and develops a
    real world vision for change in your organization.
    You will be able to implement that change through
    a specific strategy.

    *   Develop a strong comprehension of your default
        leadership style
    *   Explore where that style helps and hinders your
        leadership coaching performance
    *   Explore the components of a powerful vision
    *   Develop a vision for change

2. Remove the roadblocks –a new take on corporate
    change strategy

    It means delving deeper into your change vision.
    This focuses on the systematic and people
    challenges of change and offers a simple but

effective method for implementing change from inception to pre-implementation.

- Sharpen your change vision into an effective change initiative
- Identify roadblocks to implementing your change initiative
- Obtain tools to remove roadblocks to change
- Gain the awareness and tools to highlight corporate culture
- Empower change to drive real performance improvements

3. Lead others

You will identify how to give people what they need to create stronger relationships, increased effectiveness and a high performance workplace. People engage in change only because they want to do this, that's why you have to discover how to motivate them, because everyone is unique. You have to determine them to be responsible for their decisions or tasks and hold them accountable.

- Achieve leadership mentoring skills
- Motivate people through a set of values
- Cultivate the art of influencing

- Inspire people
- Remove the barriers between people

I hope you understood through this amount of information the importance of leadership coaching for achieving performance in an organization or team.

Thank you for purchasing and reading my book. I hope you have enjoyed it and you have received the value that I have put in it.

I have one last requirement - it won't take more than one minute, please leave an honest review.

If you liked this book, I have 2 similar books about self-development: how to create your personal and career development plan and how to discover the power within you.

http://www.amazon.com/Discover-Power-Within-Potential-Successful-ebook/dp/B00RFT1W38/ref=pd_sim_kstore_2?ie=UTF8&refRID=1V34C00TA3XH7AN9WDGK

http://www.amazon.com/Setting-Goals-Personal-Development-Plan-yourself-ebook/dp/B00RW7B7Z6/ref=sr_1_1?s=digital-text&ie=UTF8&qid=1423476650&sr=1-1&keywords=personal+development+plan`